Advanced Decision Support Tools

to accompany

INTRODUCTION TO OPERATIONS AND SUPPLY CHAIN MANAGEMENT

Advanced Decision Support Tools

to accompany

INTRODUCTION TO OPERATIONS AND SUPPLY CHAIN MANAGEMENT
Cecil C. Bozarth
Robert B. Handfield

Cecil C. Bozarth
North Carolina State University

PEARSON
Prentice Hall

Upper Saddle River, New Jersey 07458

VP/Editorial Director: Jeff Shelstad
Senior Managing Editor: Alana Bradley
Senior Editorial Assistant: Jane Avery
Manufacturing Manager: Vincent Scelta
Manager, Print Production: Christy Mahon
Production Editor & Buyer: Wanda Rockwell
Printer/Binder: Technical Communication Services

10 9 8 7 6 5 4 3
ISBN 0-13-187480-2

Advanced Decision Support Tools

Supplement A

Linear Programming

SUPPLEMENT OBJECTIVES

By the end of this supplement, you will be able to:

- Write out the objective function and constraints for a simple linear programming problem.

- Graph the two-variable linear programming problem, and identify the optimal solution.

- Build a simple linear programming problem in Excel, and solve using the Solver function.

- Use Solver's sensitivity reports to interpret the results of an Excel-based linear programming problem.

INTRODUCTION

In Chapters 11 and 13, we introduced optimization modeling and described some specific models of interest to logistics and sales and operations planning. In this supplement material, we talk in more depth about one approach to optimization modeling, linear programming. We have intentionally written this supplement so that it can be used on its own, or in addition to the above chapter material.

Optimization models are a class of mathematical models where the user seeks to optimize some objective function subject to some constraints. An **objective function** is a quantitative function that we hope to optimize (maximize or minimize). **Constraints** are quantifiable conditions that place limitations on the set of possible solutions. A solution is only acceptable if it does not break any of the constraints.

In order for optimization modeling to work, several conditions must apply:

1. The user must be able to state in mathematical terms both the objective function and constraints.

2. There must be feasible solution to the problem. For example, if total market demand is 1000 units, total supply must be greater than or equal to 1000.

3. There must be some constraints that place limits on the objective function we hope to achieve. For instance, if we want to maximize revenues, there must be resource constraints. Otherwise, we would continue to produce more and more goods and revenues would continue to grow forever. The same idea holds for minimization problems. An airline might want to minimize costs, but not at the expense of basic safety requirements.

We will begin our in-depth discussion of optimization modeling with linear programming. We will start by showing the graphical solution to the two-variable problem. The purpose of this first section will be to give you an intuitive feel for how linear programming works. We will then show how more complex optimization models can be solved and evaluated using Microsoft's Solver function.

A.1 LINEAR PROGRAMMING DEFINED

Linear programming is a special class of optimization model in which the objective function and constraints consist of linear equations. Examples of linear equations include:

Objective function: Maximize $4*A + $2.5*B

Constraints: $y = 2*x$
$z = 4*x + 5*y + 2.5*z$

Non-linear equations include:

Objective function: Maximize B*A

Constraints: $y = x^2$
$z = \sqrt{4*x + 5*y + 2.5*z}$

While there are techniques to solve non-linear optimization problems, the graphical techniques we discuss next can only be used when the objective function and constraints are expressed in linear form.

The Two-Variable Linear Programming Problem

To illustrate the various tools and techniques, we introduce the case of Nantucket Muscle Works (NMW). NMW is a small manufacture who produces two products, the "Abdominator" and the "ChestMax." The company has the determined the following:

Each Abdominator:

- Sells for $700.
- Requires 10 hours of assembly and 3 hours of painting.
- Has a maximum weekly demand of 25 units.

Each ChestMax:

- Sells for $500.
- Requires 8 hours of assembly and 6 hours of painting.
- Has a maximum weekly demand of only 15 units.

In addition, there are 200 hours of assembly time available each week, and 84 hours of painting time available each week. Furthermore, management has decided that it will not hold finished goods inventory. Therefore, the company will produce no more than it can sell in any given week.

Management would like to know how many units of each product it should make each week in order to maximize revenues. To translate this problem into linear programming terms, we will need to write out the objective function and the constraints. The objective function is to maximize revenues:

$$\text{Maximize: } \$700A + \$500C \qquad\qquad [A-1]$$

Where:

A = the number of Abdominators made
C = the number of ChestMaxes made

Next, come the constraints. There are two resource constraints (assembly and painting) and two demand constraints (one for each product):

Assembly constraint:	$10A + 8C \leq 200$	[A-2]
Printing constraint:	$3A + 6C \leq 84$	[A-3]
Abdominator demand constraint:	$A \leq 25$	[A-4]
ChestMax demand constraint:	$C \leq 15$	[A-5]

There are a couple of interesting things to note about the problem formulation. First, A and C are the two **decision variables** that will be manipulated to find the best solution. Second, notice the "$\leq$" sign in each of the constraints. If, in the final solution, the left hand is equal to the right hand of the constraint, then we say the constraint is a **binding** constraint. Otherwise, it is a **non-binding** constraint. As we shall see, we will want to continue improving the objective function until one or more of the constraints becomes binding.

The Graphical Method

For a problem with two decision variables, we can represent the problem graphically. The steps are as follows:

1. Convert the constraints into equalities and then plot them on a graph.
2. Mark off the region on the graph that contains combinations of decision variables that still satisfy all of the constraints. This is known as the feasible region.
3. Calculate the objective function for each corner point of the feasible region. The optimal solution will be identified by the point(s) that maximize / minimize the objective function.

Step 1: Convert and plot the constraints. For our sample problem, converting the constraints into equalities gives the following:

$$10A + 8C = 200 \text{ (Assembly constraint)}$$
$$A + 6C = 84 \text{ (Painting constraint)}$$
$$A = 25 \text{ (Abdominator demand constraint)}$$
$$C = 15 \text{ (ChestMax demand constraint)}$$

The resulting graph is shown in Figure A.1. To illustrate how we graphed these constraints, let's take the assembly constraint, $10A + 8C = 200$ and find the two end points.

Setting A = 0:

10(0) + 8C = 200,   C = 25

Setting C = 0:

10A + 8(0) = 200,   A = 20

Drawing a line between the points (0,25) and (20,0) identifies all values of (A, C) that equal 200. The remaining constraints are graphed in a similar fashion.

Figure A.1: Constraints for NMW Problem

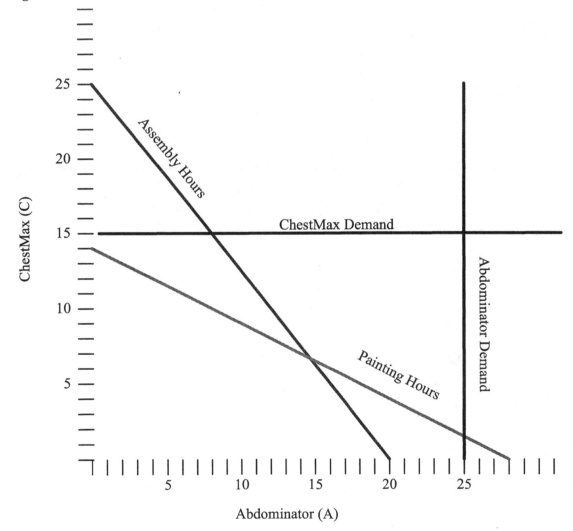

Step 2: Mark off the Feasible Region. The feasible region contains all combinations of A and C (the decision variables) that satisfy the constraints.   Figure A.2 shows the shaded feasible region for our sample problem. Note that the two demand constraints *do not* intersect with the feasible region. For this particular problem, then, we can say that these constraints are **redundant**. That is, they have no effect on the feasible region.

Figure A.2: Feasible region for NMW Problem

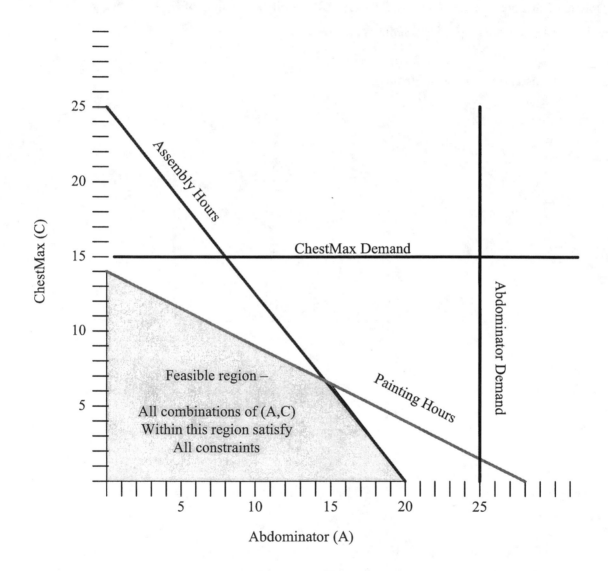

Step 3. Calculate the objective function for each corner point in the feasible region, and identify the optimal solution. For the two variable linear programming problem, it is a general truth that the optimal solution – i.e., the one that results in the best objective function value – will lie at one of the corner points of the feasible region. Table A.1 shows the four corner points in our sample problem:

Table A.1

Abdominators	ChestMaxes
0	0
20	0
0	14
14.67	6.67

The last set of corner point values, (14.67, 6.67) occurs where the assembly and painting constraints cross. To find the values of A and C, we will use simple algebra to first solve for one decision variable, and then the other. Solving for C:

$$-3 * (10A + 8C = 200) \quad = \quad -30A - 24C = -600$$
$$10*(3A + 6C = 84) \quad = \quad +\underline{\quad 30A + 60C = 840}$$
$$36C = 240$$
$$\mathbf{C = 6.67}$$

And solving for A:

$$10A + 8*(\mathbf{6.67}) = 200$$
$$\mathbf{A = 14.67}$$

You might have noticed that these last corner point values are fractional, and in fact linear programming can give such results, even when the decision variable in reality must be a whole value. When this occurs, decision-makers will often round to the closest whole numbers. Table A.2 shows the objective function value for each of the corner points. According to the table, the optimal solution is to make 20 Abdominators and 0 ChestMaxes, for a total revenue of $1400.

Table A.2

Abdominators	ChestMaxes	Objective Function: $700A + $500C
0	0	$0
20	**0**	**$14,000**
0	14	$7,000
14.67	6.67	$13,600

Looking at Figure A.3, we can also see that the optimal solution (20, 0) sits on the assembly hours constraint line. What this means is that in order to produce 20 Abdominators and 0 ChestMaxes, we will need all available assembly hours. The math verifies this:

(10 assembly hours) * (20 Abdominators) = 200 assembly hours

In contrast, the optimal solution does not lie on the painting hours constraint line:

(3 painting hours) * (20 Abdominators) = 60 painting hours.

In linear programming terms, the assembly hours constraint is **binding**, while the painting hours constraint is **non-binding**.

Figure A.3: Optimal solution for NMW Problem

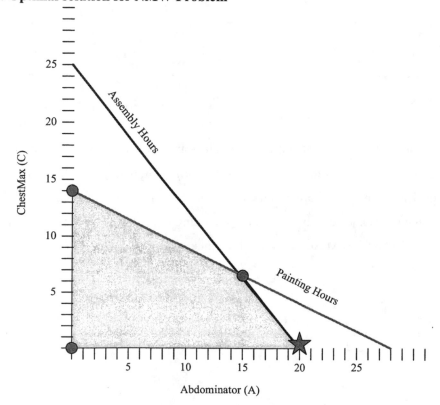

****

Boxed Example A.1: Cost Minimization at Trusty Dog Food

Each bag of Trusty Dog Food must contain, at a minimum, 72 grams of Nutrient A and 40 grams of Nutrient B. The company that produces Trusty Dog Food has two sources for these nutrients: Ingredients M and N. Information on these two ingredients follows:

Ingredient	Grams of Nutrient A, per ounce	Grams of Nutrient B, per ounce	Maximum ounces per bag	Cost per ounce
M	4	8	10	$0.29
N	6	2	15	$0.20

Because taste is a consideration, the company has decided that no bag should contain more than 10 or 15 ounces of Ingredients M and N, respectively. Given these nutritional and taste requirements, the company would like to minimize the ingredient costs. In linear programming terms, the problem can be stated as follows:

$$\text{Minimize: } \$0.29M + \$0.20N$$

Where:

M = Ounces of Ingredient M required

N = Ounces of Ingredient N required

Nutrient A constraint:	$4M + 6N \geq 72$
Nutrient B constraint:	$8M + 2N \geq 40$
Ingredient M constraint:	$M \leq 10$
Ingredient N constraint:	$N \leq 15$

Because this is a cost minimization problem, the graphical result looks a little different than before (Figure A.4). The feasible region is up and to the right of the nutrient constraints, and below and to the left of the ingredient constraints. But the key point is that the feasible region is **bounded**, meaning there is a finite solution to the problem.

Investigation shows that the optimal solution is at the corner point (2.4, 10.4). Specifically:

M = 2.4 ounces

N = 10.4 ounces

Total Nutrient A = 4M + 6N = 72 grams

Total Nutrient B = 8M + 2N = 40 grams

Total cost = ($0.29)*2.4 + ($0.20)*10.4 = $2.776

Figure A.4: Graphical solution for Trusty Dog Food Problem

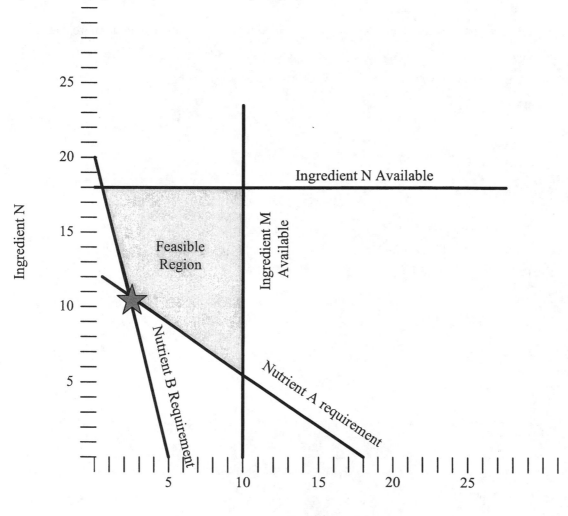

****

Computer-Based Solutions

While the graphical method is easy to understand and useful for demonstrating the basic principles behind linear programming, it is impractical for models involving more than two decision variables. When this is the case, we need to turn to computer-based methods.

Advances in computer technology have dramatically increased the size and complexity of models that can be solved. Models with hundreds of variables that used to take hours to solve on the largest mainframe computers can now be solved in a matter of minutes or even seconds on desktop or laptop computers. In this section, we will show how such models can be solved and interpreted using Microsoft Excel's Solver function. Solver is available as an add-on function for Excel. Once it has been installed, it can be accessed through the "Tools" drop-down menu.

Returning to our Nantucket Muscle Works (NMW) example, the first step in using Excel's Solver is to build the objective function, resource requirements, and constraint information into an Excel spreadsheet. Figure A.5 shows one possible layout.

Figure A.5: Excel spreadsheet for NMW Problem

	A	B	C	D	E	F
1	**Allocating Capacity to Maximize Revenue**					
2						
3	Revenue:	$ -				
4					Maximum	
5		***Labor Requirements***			that can be	Actual
6		Assembly	Painting	Price	sold in week	Production
7	Abdominators	10	3	$ 700	25	0
8	ChestMaxes	8	6	$ 500	15	0
9						
10		Hours	Actual	Slack		
11		Available	Hours	Hours		
12	Assembly	200	0	200		
13	Painting	84	0	84		

Some of the cells contain parameter values (capacity limits, demand limits, etc.) while other cells contain formulas. Cells F7 and F8 contain the values for our two decision variables, A and C. The Solver program will eventually determine the optimal values and place them in these cells. The cells with formulas include:

B3 = Objective function = D7*F7 + D8*F8

C12 = Actual assembly hours used = B7*F7+B8*F8

C13 = Actual painting hours used = C7*F7 + C8+F8

D13 = Slack hours in assembly = B12 – C12

D13 = Slack hours in painting = B13 – C13

Once we have laid out the problem in the spreadsheet, the next step is to define the linear programming model in Solver. That is, we must explicitly tell Solver where the objective function is and what the constraints are, using the cells and equations in the spreadsheet.

Figure 6 shows the spreadsheet with the Solver dialog box. The "Target Cell" is our objective function, Cell B3. Just below, we have clicked "max" to indicate we want a solution that maximizes the value in Cell B3. Below that, there is a space labeled "By Changing Cells:". Here, we tell Solver where our decision variables are located.

Below that is a list of all the constraints that must be met. The first constraint, *$C$12:$C$13<=$B$12:$B$13,* ensures that total assembly and painting hours used do not exceed capacity. Similarly, *$F$7:$F$8<=$E$7:$E$8* ensures that actual production for the Abdominator or ChestMax do not exceed the demand limits.

Finally, we include a new constraint, *$F$7:$F$8>=0.* To understand where this constraint comes from, look back at Figure 2. Notice that our feasible region assumed that we would not allow negative units of production. While this makes intuitive sense to *us*, we need to be explicit when using a computer to solve the problem. Specifically, if we allow negative decision variable values, Solver may conclude that it can "find" additional assembly and painting time by "making" negative ChestMaxes! This last constraint ensures that the solution we get is not only feasible from a mathematical perspective, but from a business perspective as well.

Figure A.6: Spreadsheet and Solver dialog box for NMW Problem

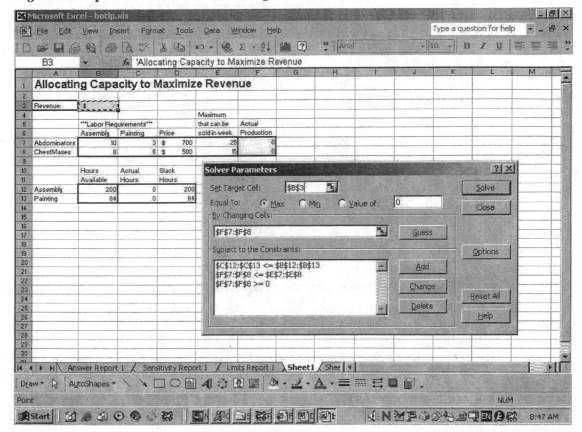

Once we have completely defined the linear programming model to Solver, we can find a solution by clicking the "Solve" button in the dialog box. Figure A.7 shows the updated spreadsheet. Figures A.8 and A.9 show optional output reports generated by Solver. We will go through each one of these in detail.

As you can see in Figure A.7, we get the same solution as before – produce 20 Abdominators and use up all the assembly time, resulting in revenues of $14,000. Furthermore, the solution uses all of the assembly hours, but still have 24 hours of painting available. Again, this is consistent with what we saw in Figure A.3.

Figure A.7: Optimal solution for NMW Problem

**** Allocating capacity to maximize profits *****					
Revenue:	$ 14,000				
	Labor Requirements			Maximum that can be sold in week	Actual Production
	Assembly	Painting	Price		
Abdominators	10	3	$ 700	25	20
ChestMaxes	8	6	$ 500	15	0
	Hours Available	Actual Hours	Slack Hours		
Assembly	200	200	0		
Painting	84	60	24		

The answer report in Figure A.8 was generated by Solver, and contains much the same information shown in Figure A.7. According to this report, two constraints were binding: available assembly hours and non-negative production of ChestMaxes. What this tells us is that if we had not forced ChestMax production to be non-negative, Solver might have tried to "produce" negative ChestMaxes to "free up" additional assembly time.

Sensitivity Reports

Perhaps the most interesting Solver report is the sensitivity report, shown in Figure A.9. In general, the "Reduced Gradient" tells us what impact increasing each of the decision by one unit would have on the objective function. For our sample problem, attempting to produce one more Abdominator is infeasible; therefore, the reduced gradient = 0. We could produce one ChestMax, but only by stealing resources away from Abdominator production. If we were to "force" production of one ChestMax, the reduced gradient value tells us the objective function would be lowered by $60.

Notice the "Lagrange Multiplier" values associated with assembly and painting hours. More commonly known as **shadow prices**, the Lagrange multipliers show the marginal improvement to the objective function of an additional unit of resource. So according to the sensitivity report, one additional hour of assembly time would increase revenues by $70. But since we had extra painting time available, any additional hours here would make no difference (Lagrange Multiplier = 0).

A word of caution: The reduced gradient and Lagrange multiplier values are only valid for *small* changes from the current solution. For instance, we can continue to add assembly hours until it no longer becomes a binding constraint, at which point the Lagrange multiplier for assembly hours would drop to 0.

To visualize this, imagine shifting the assembly constraint line in Figure A.3 up and to the right until it no longer forms an edge of the feasible region.

When we *increase* the right-hand side of a "≤" constraint, or *decrease* the right-hand of a ">" constraint, we are said to be **relaxing the constraint**. In general, relaxing a constraint will have one of two effects:

- The solution will improve because the constraint is binding.
- The solution will not change because the constraint is non-binding.

Conversely, *decreasing* the right-hand side of a "≤" constraint, or *increasing* the right-hand of a "≥" constraint will only serve to shrink the size of the feasible region, with one of two possible outcomes:

- The solution will degrade because the constraint is binding.
- The solution will not change because the constraint is non-binding.

So in summary, relaxing a constraint can only help the solution; tightening it up can only hurt the solution.

Figure A.8: Solver answer report for NMW problem

Microsoft Excel 10.0 Answer Report
Worksheet: [botlp.xls]Sheet1
Report Created: 2/2/2005 8:57:34 AM

Target Cell (Max)

Cell	Name	Original Value	Final Value
$B$3	Revenue:	$ -	$ 14,000

Adjustable Cells

Cell	Name	Original Value	Final Value
$F$7	Abdominators Production	0	20
$F$8	ChestMaxes Production	0	0

Constraints

Cell	Name	Cell Value	Formula	Status	Slack
$C$12	Assembly Hours	200	$C$12<=$B$12	Binding	0
$C$13	Painting Hours	60	$C$13<=$B$13	Not Binding	24
$F$7	Abdominators Production	20	$F$7>=0	Not Binding	20
$F$8	ChestMaxes Production	0	$F$8>=0	Binding	0
$F$7	Abdominators Production	20	$F$7<=$E$7	Not Binding	5
$F$8	ChestMaxes Production	0	$F$8<=$E$8	Not Binding	15

Figure A.9: Solver sensitivity report for NMW problem

Microsoft Excel 10.0 Sensitivity Report
Worksheet: [botlp.xls]Sheet1
Report Created: 2/2/2005 8:48:44 AM

Adjustable Cells

Cell	Name	Final Value	Reduced Gradient
$F$7	Abdominators Production	20	0
$F$8	ChestMaxes Production	0	-60

Constraints

Cell	Name	Final Value	Lagrange Multiplier
$C$12	Assembly Hours	200	70
$C$13	Painting Hours	60	0

****

Boxed Example A.2: The QuadPopper Problem

After several months of making only Abdominators and ChestMaxes, NMW introduces a new product, the QuadPopper. Each QuadPopper requires 5 hours of assembly and 5 hours of painting time, and sells for $650. The maximum number of QuadPoppers that can be sold in a week is 20.

At the same time, NMV has doubled its assembly and painting time capacities to 400 and 168 hours, respectively. What is the new product mix that will maximize weekly revenues?

Figure A.10 shows the updated spreadsheet and Solver dialog box. As you can see, the objective function in Cell B3 has been modified to include the QuadPopper. The spreadsheet also has a new decision variable in Cell F9.

Figure A.10: Excel problem for extended NMW problem

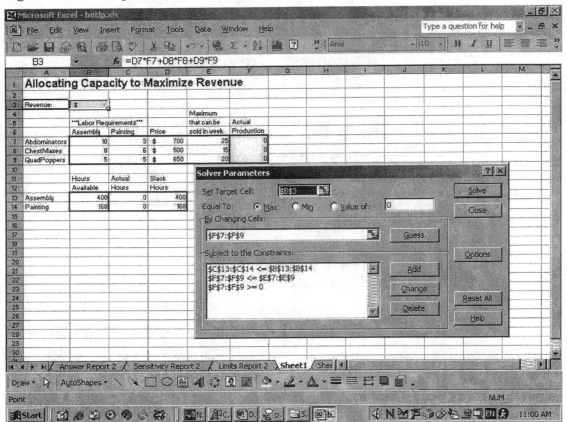

The new solution is shown in Figure A.11. The new optimal solution is to make 25 Abdominators, 15 ChestMaxes, and 18.6 QuadPoppers, for a total revenue of $37,090. In reality, NMV cannot make partial units, so they would likely end up producing just 18 QuadPoppers, and total revenue would be slightly less at $36,700.

Figure A.11: Optimal solution to extended NMW problem

	A	B	C	D	E	F
1	**Allocating Capacity to Maximize Revenue**					
2						
3	Revenue:	$ 37,090				
4					Maximum	
5		***Labor Requirements***			that can be	Actual
6		Assembly	Painting	Price	sold in week	Production
7	Abdominators	10	3	$ 700	25	25
8	ChestMaxes	8	6	$ 500	15	15
9	QuadPoppers	5	5	$ 650	20	18.6
10						
11		Hours	Actual	Slack		
12		Available	Hours	Hours		
13	Assembly	400	343	57		
14	Painting	168	168	0		

The sensitivity report (Figure A.12) suggests that increasing the incremental demand for Abdominators and ChestMaxes would increase revenues by $310 and $500, respectively. At the same time, painting is now the resource constraint; not assembly as before. An additional hour of painting time would allow NMV to increase revenues by $130.

Figure A.12: Sensitivity report for extended NMW problem

Microsoft Excel 10.0 Sensitivity Report
Worksheet: [botlp.xls]Sheet1
Report Created: 2/2/2005 11:05:58 AM

Adjustable Cells

Cell	Name	Final Value	Reduced Gradient
$F$7	Abdominators Production	25	310
$F$8	ChestMaxes Production	15	500
$F$9	QuadPoppers Production	18.6	0

Constraints

Cell	Name	Final Value	Lagrange Multiplier
$C$13	Assembly Hours	343	0
$C$14	Painting Hours	168	130

****

A.2 SENSITIVITY ANALYSIS

Business situations are rarely static. Demand levels can change; resources can be expanded or contracted; prices can change. Because of this, decision-makers are rarely satisfied with determining the solution for just a single set of inputs. Rather, decision-makers also want to see how sensitive the solution to an optimization problem is to changes in the underlying constraints and objective function. A **robust solution** is one that is affected little or none at all when reasonable changes are made to the parameters in the objective function and constraints.

One way to understand the impact of such changes is through sensitivity reports. Consider the sensitivity reports shown in Figures 9 and 12. These showed the value of additional units or resources (the LaGrange multipliers, or shadow prices) and the impact of changes to the decision variables (reduced gradient).

Another way to evaluate solutions is to make selected changes to the objective function and constraints, and see what impact this has on the solution. In the following example, we show an example of how this can be done.

****

Boxed Example 3: Sensitivity Analysis at Trusty Dog Food

In Boxed Example A.1, the cost minimizing solution was to include 2.4 ounces of Ingredient M and 10.4 ounces of Ingredient N in each bag of dog food. This solution would meet the nutritional requirements at the minimum cost, without exceeding the limits placed on either of the ingredients.

After generating this solution, management began to wonder what impact changes to the ingredients' costs would have on the optimal solution. To address this question, management asked the purchasing department to identify a likely range of costs for the two key ingredients, M and N (Table A.3):

Table A.3: Ingredient costs, Trusty Dog Food problem

Ingredient	Expected cost per ounce	Maximum cost per ounce	Minimum price per ounce
M	$0.29	$0.32	$0.26
N	$0.20	$0.22	$0.18

To evaluate the impact of cost changes, management has decided to use Excel's Solver function to see how the solution changes as the costs change. Table A.4 identifies nine possible cost scenarios. Scenario 5 is the current state. Scenario 3 represents a situation where Ingredient M is at its lowest cost and Ingredient N is at its maximum. Conversely, Scenario 7 has Ingredient M at its highest cost and Ingredient N at its lowest.

Table A.4: Cost scenarios to be evaluated

Scenario	Ingredient M	Ingredient N
1	$0.26	$0.18
2	$0.26	$0.20
3	**$0.26**	**$0.22**
4	$0.29	$0.18
5	**$0.29**	**$0.20**
6	$0.29	$0.22
7	**$0.32**	**$0.18**
8	$0.32	$0.20
9	$0.32	$0.22

Figure A.13 shows the spreadsheet and the Solver dialog box for the Trusty Dog Food problem. The constraints are the same as those listed in Boxed Example A.1.

Figure A.13: Excel spreadsheet and Solver dialog box for Trusty Dog Food problem

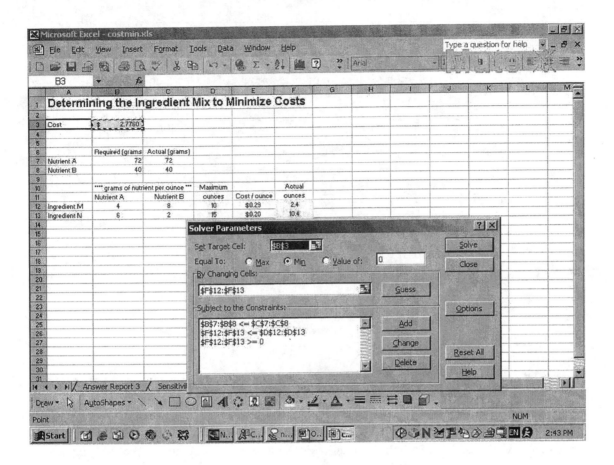

Resolving the spreadsheet for the nine cost scenarios listed in Table A.4 yields the results shown in Table A.5. The results are telling: Even though the optimal cost per bag of dog food will change, the optimal mix of ingredients remains stable across the range of costs. Based on this information, management feels confident that their decision to go with 2.4 ounces of Ingredient M and 10.4 ounces of Ingredient N is a robust solution.

Table A.5: Optimal solutions for various cost scenarios, Trusty Dog Food problem

			Resulting Solver Solution		
Scenario	Ingredient M	Ingredient N	Optimal amount of M	Optimal amount of N	Optimal Cost per bag
1	$0.26	$0.18	2.4	10.4	$2.496
2	$0.26	$0.20	2.4	10.4	$2.704
3	$0.26	$0.22	2.4	10.4	$2.912
4	$0.29	$0.18	2.4	10.4	$2.568
5	$0.29	$0.20	2.4	10.4	$2.776
6	$0.29	$0.22	2.4	10.4	$2.984
7	$0.32	$0.18	2.4	10.4	$2.640
8	$0.32	$0.20	2.4	10.4	$2.848
0	$0.32	$0.22	2.4	10.4	$3.056

****

SUMMARY

In this supplement, we discussed optimization modeling in more depth. We demonstrated the graphical solution to the two-variable linear programming problem for both a revenue maximization and cost minimization problem, and showed how such problems can be easily solved using Excel's Solver function. Last, we discussed the importance of sensitivity analysis, and why decision makers need to understand how the solution may change as underlying assumptions and constraints change.

DISCUSSION QUESTIONS

1. Figures 2 and 3 show the bounded feasible region for the Nantucket Muscle Works problem. Now suppose there (Figures 1 – 3) wanted to maximize revenues, but there were no limits on resources or demand. What would the feasible region look like? Use this example to explain what is meant by an unbounded problem.

2. In the text, we defined a robust solution as one that is affected little or none at all when reasonable changes are made to the parameters in the objective function and constraints. What do you think we mean by "reasonable?" What would be an unreasonable change? Who would decide? Give examples using either the NMW or Trusty Dog Food examples.

3. What are the advantages of using structured approaches like linear programming to evaluate business problems? What are some of the limitations? Can you think of a situation where it might make sense to use managerial judgement to "override" an optimal solution?

4. Consider Boxed Example 2. Suppose we expand the demand for QuadPoppers. Is this an example of relaxing or tightening a constraint? Based on the results in Boxed Example 2, would you expect the solution to change? Why or why not?

PROBLEMS

Additional homework problems are available at http://www.prenhall.com/bozarth. These problems use Excel to generate customized problems for different class sections or even different students.

(* = easy; ** = moderate; *** = advanced)

1. (**) Consider the Trusty Dog Food example in Boxed Example A.1. Suppose management has decided to position Trusty Dog Food as a premium brand. As such, they would like to maximize nutritional value while not exceeding the limits on Ingredients M and N, and not exceeding a cost of $4.00 for these two ingredients. Rewrite the objective functions and constraints to solve this new problem.

Use the following information for Problems 2 through 5.

The XYZ Company makes two different products, described below:

Product	Selling Price	Maximum Weekly Demand	Amount of Material A needed	Amount of Material B needed
A10	$20	30	8	9
B20	$25	20	10	6
C30	$30	75	14	12

XYZ cannot store finished goods. Therefore, whatever is made in any one week must be sold in that week. The maximum amount of Material A and Material B available in any one week is 250 and 300 units, respectively.

2. (*) Write out the objective function for the above problem. Is this a maximization or minimization problem?

3. (***) Develop an Excel spreadsheet to solve the above problem, using the Solver function. How can we ensure that the Solver function does not make "negative" products? What is the optimal solution to the problem? What are the binding constraints? What are the LaGrange multipliers associated with these constraints? Interpret.

4. (**) Suppose the maximum weekly demand for each of the three products is 10 units. How does this change the optimal solution? Is this an example of tightening or relaxing the constraints?

5. (**) Refer back to the original problem. Suppose XYZ has unlimited access to materials. How might you modify the spreadsheet to solve this problem **without** removing the constraints defined in Solver? – After all, we want to leave the spreadsheet "intact" in case material constraints do arise in the future. (Hint: Think about putting "big numbers" in the spreadsheet cells.). Resolve the problem with unlimited access to materials. What is/are the binding constraint(s)?

Supplement B

Waiting Line Theory and Simulation Modeling

Supplement Objectives

Introduction

B.1 Waiting Lines

    Alternative environments

    Assumptions behind waiting line theory

    Waiting line formulas for three different environments

B.2 Simulation Modeling

    Monte Carlo simulation

    Building and evaluating simulation models with SimQuick

Supplement Summary

Discussion Questions

Problems

SUPPLEMENT OBJECTIVES

By the end of this supplement, you will be able to:

- Describe different types of waiting line systems.
- Use statistics-based formulas to estimate waiting line lengths and waiting times for three different types of waiting line systems.
- Explain the purpose, advantages and disadvantages, and steps of simulation modeling.
- Develop a simple Monte Carlo simulation using Microsoft Excel.
- Develop and analyze a system using SimQuick.

INTRODUCTION

Chapter 8 introduced waiting line theory and provided some formulas for calculating waiting times and line lengths for a simple waiting line situation. In this supplement, we describe two addition waiting line environments, and demonstrate how statistically-derived formulas can be used to assess the performance of these systems as well.

The second half of this supplement introduces simulation modeling. Simulation is often described in conjunction with waiting lines because many complex waiting line systems cannot be analyzed through neatly derived formulas. That said, simulation can be used in any environment where actual occurrences of interest – arrivals, quality problems, work times, etc. – can be modeled mathematically. We show how Monte Carlo simulation can be used to develop a very simple simulation using Excel. We then use one particular simulation package, SimQuick, to illustrate simulation model building and analysis.

B.1 WAITING LINES

As we noted in Chapter 8, many service and manufacturing processes include waiting lines where people or items must wait before being processed. In such environments, waiting lines can have a dramatic impact on the time it takes to complete the process. Waiting line theory helps managers evaluate the relationship between capacity decisions and such important performance issues as waiting times and line lengths.

Alternative Environments

In Chapter 8, we illustrated how waiting line theory worked using the example of a waiting line environment in which there was a single path through the one process step, and both the arrival rate and service rate were probabilistic. In the language of waiting line theory, this is known as a **single channel, single phase system** (Figure B.1).

Figure B.1 Single channel, single phase system

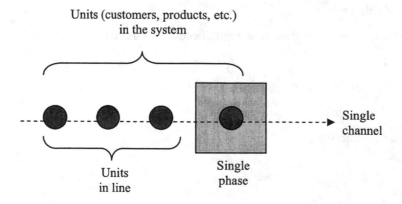

We then illustrated how statistics-based formulas could be used to answer questions such as:

- What percentage of the time will the process be busy?
- On average, *how long* will a unit have to wait in line? How long will it be in the system (waiting and being served)?
- On average, *how many* units will be in line?
- How will these averages be affected by the arrival rate of units and the service rate at the process step?

Obviously, there are many waiting line environments that do not fit this mold. For example, an automatic car wash may have one line and one process step, but the service time is *constant*. Or we may be interested in a multi-channel, single-phase system, such as a bank. Here, there is only one process step, but there can be multiple paths through the system, depending on how many tellers are working (Figure B.2).

Figure B.2 Multiple channel, single phase system

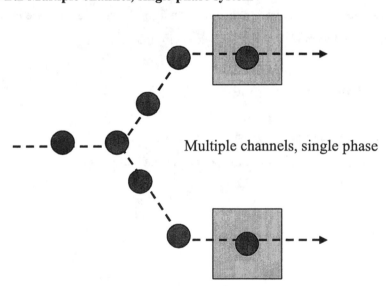

Multiple channels, single phase

Or we may be interested in a single channel, multiple phase system. Examples include a hospital emergency room, where you wait to check in (phase 1), and then you wait to see a doctor or nurse (phase 2). Figure B.3 illustrates such a system.

Another common example is at some fast food drive-up restaurants, where you place an order, pay for your food at the first window, then pick up your food at the last window. In this case, there are three phases. Finally, we can even have multiple channel, multiple phase systems. In general, the more complex the environment is, the less likely we are to be able to analyze it with pre-established formulas.

Figure B.3: Single channel, multiple phase system

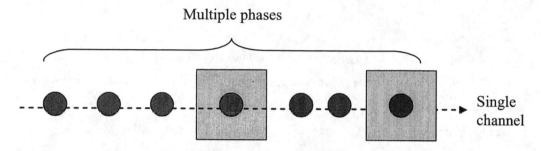

In the remainder of this section, we review some of the key assumptions and terminology that make up waiting line theory, and introduce some formulas for determining waiting line performance for two additional waiting line environments – the single channel, single phase system with constant service times, and the multiple channel, single phase system. In the second half of the supplement, we introduce simulation modeling, which can be used to model more complex environments.

Assumptions Behind Waiting Line Theory

Arrivals. In most waiting line models, customers are assumed to arrive at random intervals, based on a Poisson distribution. The probability of n arrivals in T time periods is calculated as follows:

$$P_n = \frac{(\lambda T)^n}{n!} e^{-\lambda T} \qquad\qquad \text{[B-1]}$$

Where:

P_n = Probability of n arrivals in T time periods

$\lambda.$ = Arrival rate

T = Number of time periods

Service times. Similarly, waiting line models assume that service times will either be constant or vary. In the latter case, modelers often use the exponential distribution to model service times, using the symbol μ to refer to the service rate.

Other assumptions. Finally, we need to make some assumptions about the order in which customers are served, the size of the customer population, and whether or not customers can balk or renege. All waiting line formulas assume that customers are served on a first-come, first served (FCFS) basis. Other priority rules might consider the urgency of the customers' needs (as in an emergency room), the speed with which customers can be served, or even the desirability of different customer types. In addition, we will assume that the population of customers is effectively infinite; that is, we are not likely to run through all the possible customers any time soon.

Last, we will assume that customers enter the system and remain there until they are served, regardless of the length of the line or time spent waiting. They neither balk (decide against entering the system to begin with) nor renege (leave the line after entering).

Waiting Line Formulas for Three Different Environments

Table B.1 contains formulas for estimating performance in three different waiting line environments. In all three cases, the formulas require that we know:

- The average number of arrivals per period of time, λ
- The average time each server takes to service a unit, μ

The first row of formulas is for a single-channel, single-phase system with probabilistic arrivals and service times. The second row is for a single-channel, single-phase system in which service times are constant. The third row described a multiple-channel, single-phase system (Figure B.2). We illustrate how these formulas can be used in Examples B.1 through B.3.

Table B.1: Waiting line formulas for three different environments

Waiting line environment: λ = average number of arrivals per period of time μ = average time each server takes to service a unit M = Number of channels	Average number of units waiting, C_w	Average number of units in system, C_S	Average time spent waiting, T_w	Average time spent in system, T_S
Single channel, single phase with Poisson arrivals and exponential service times	$\dfrac{\lambda^2}{\mu(\mu-\lambda)}$ [B-2]	$C_w + \dfrac{\lambda}{\mu}$ [B-3]	$\dfrac{\lambda}{\mu(\mu-\lambda)}$ [B-4]	$T_w + \dfrac{1}{\mu}$ [B-5]
Single channel, single phase with Poisson arrivals and <u>constant</u> service times	$\dfrac{\lambda^2}{2\mu(\mu-\lambda)}$ [B-6]	$C_w + \dfrac{\lambda}{\mu}$ [B-7]	$\dfrac{\lambda}{2\mu(\mu-\lambda)}$ [B-8]	$T_w + \dfrac{1}{\mu}$ [B-9]
Multiple channel, single phase with Poisson arrivals and exponential service times ("multi-server model") where: P_0 = Probability of 0 units in the system = $\dfrac{1}{\left[\sum\limits_{n=0}^{M-1}\frac{1}{n!}\left(\frac{\lambda}{\mu}\right)^n\right]+\frac{1}{M!}\left(\frac{\lambda}{\mu}\right)^M\left(\frac{M\mu}{M\mu-\lambda}\right)}$ [B-10]	$C_S - \dfrac{\lambda}{\mu}$ [B-11]	$\dfrac{\lambda\mu\left(\frac{\lambda}{\mu}\right)^M}{(M-1)!(M\mu-\lambda)^2}P_0 + \left(\frac{\lambda}{\mu}\right)$ [B-12]	$T_S - \dfrac{1}{\mu}$ [B-13]	$\dfrac{\mu\left(\frac{\lambda}{\mu}\right)^M}{(M-1)!(M\mu-\lambda)^2}P_0 + \left(\frac{1}{\mu}\right)$ [B-14]

****

Boxed Example B.1: Luc's Deluxe Car Wash, Part 1 -- Probabilistic Arrivals and Service Times

Luc Shields, an enterprising high school student, runs a car wash where he has a single crew of workers wash cars by hand (i.e., a single-channel, single-phase system). Cars arrive about every 8 minutes, on average. Luc's crew can wash, on average, one car every 6 minutes. Arrivals follow a Poisson distribution, and the service times are exponentially distributed.

Luc would like to estimate 1) the average number of cars waiting and in the system, and 2) the average time a car spends waiting and in the system. From the information provided, we know that:

$$\text{Arrival rate} = \lambda = \frac{60 \text{ minutes}}{8 \text{ minutes}} = 7.5 \text{ cars per hour}$$

$$\text{Service rate} = \mu = \frac{60 \text{ minutes}}{6 \text{ minutes}} = 10 \text{ cars per hour}$$

Therefore, applying Equations [B-2] through [B-5]:

$$\text{Average number of cars waiting } (C_w) = \frac{\lambda^2}{\mu(\mu - \lambda)} = \frac{7.5^2}{10(10 - 7.5)} = 2.25 \text{ cars}$$

$$\text{Average number of cars in the system } (C_S) = C_w + \frac{\lambda}{\mu} = 2.25 + 0.75 = 3 \text{ cars}$$

$$\text{Average time a car spends waiting } (T_w) = \frac{\lambda}{\mu(\mu - \lambda)}$$

$$= \frac{7.5}{10(10 - 7.5)} \qquad = \qquad 0.3 \text{ hours, or about 18 minutes}$$

$$\text{Average time a car spends in the system } (T_S) = T_w + \frac{1}{\mu}$$

$$= 0.3 + 0.1 \qquad = \qquad 0.4 \text{ hours, or about 24 minutes}$$

****

****

Boxed Example B.2: Luc's Deluxe Car Wash, Part 2 -- Probabilistic Arrivals and Constant Service Times

Luc is contemplating replacing his work crew with an automated car wash system. Although the automated system is no faster than the current work crew, it can handle cars at a *constant* rate of one car every six minutes. Luc is not sure if this would make any difference with regard to the waiting line performance at his car wash, so he decides to use the equations in Table B.1 to find out.

Notice that the arrival rate and service rate are still 7.5 cars and 10 cars per hour, respectively. The difference is that the service rate no longer follows an exponential distribution, but is constant. Applying Equations [B-6] through [B-9], Luc gets the following estimates:

Average number of cars waiting $(C_w) = \dfrac{\lambda^2}{2\mu(\mu-\lambda)} = \dfrac{7.5^2}{20(10-7.5)} = 1.125$ cars

Average number of cars in the system $(C_S) = C_w + \dfrac{\lambda}{\mu} = 1.125 + 0.75 = 1.875$ cars

Average time a car spends waiting $(T_w) = \dfrac{\lambda}{2\mu(\mu-\lambda)}$

$= \dfrac{7.5}{20(10-7.5)}$ $=$ 0.15 hours, or about 9 minutes

Average time a car spends in the system $(T_S) = T_w + \dfrac{1}{\mu}$

$= 0.15 + 0.10$ $=$ 0.25 hours, or about 15 minutes

Looking at the results, Luc is surprised to see that average number of cars waiting and average time waiting are cut in half. The results impress upon Luc the impact of variability on process performance and capacity requirements.

****

****

Boxed Example B.3: Luc's Deluxe Car Wash, Part 3 -- Adding a Second Crew

Even though Luc likes the fact that an automated car wash system with constant service time would decrease waiting times and line lengths, he doesn't feel he can afford the investment at this point. Rather, Luc is thinking about adding a second crew. This would effectively make his car wash a multiple-channel, single-phase system, where M = 2. Assuming that the second crew has the same service rate numbers as the first ($\mu = 10$; service times are exponentially distributed), Luc can estimate the performance of the system using Equations [B-10] through [B-14]. To use these equations, we must first calculate the probability of zero cars in the system:

$$P_0 = \cfrac{1}{\left[\displaystyle\sum_{n=0}^{M-1}\frac{1}{n!}\left(\frac{\lambda}{\mu}\right)^n\right] + \frac{1}{M!}\left(\frac{\lambda}{\mu}\right)^M\left(\frac{M\mu}{M\mu-\lambda}\right)}$$

$$= \cfrac{1}{\left[1+\frac{7.5}{10}\right] + \frac{1}{2!}\left(\frac{7.5}{10}\right)^2\left(\frac{2*10}{2*10-7.5}\right)}$$

$$= \cfrac{1}{1.75+\frac{1}{2}(0.5625)(1.6)} = \frac{1}{1.75+0.45} = 0.4545$$

Plugging the resulting P_0 value into the formula for C_S:

$$C_S = \frac{\lambda\mu\left(\frac{\lambda}{\mu}\right)^M}{(M-1)!(M\mu-\lambda)^2}P_0 + \left(\frac{\lambda}{\mu}\right) = \frac{7.5*10\left(\frac{7.5}{10}\right)^2}{(2*10-7.5)^2}*(0.4545)+(7.5/10)$$

$$= \frac{42.1875}{25}*(0.4545)+(7.5/10) = \quad 1.517 \text{ cars in the system, on average}$$

The average number of cars waiting:

$$C_w \quad = \quad C_S - \frac{\lambda}{\mu} \quad = \quad 1.517 - 0.75 = 0.1227 \text{ cars}$$

The average time a car spends in the system:

$$T_S \quad = \quad \frac{\mu\left(\dfrac{\lambda}{\mu}\right)^M}{(M-1)!\,(M\mu-\lambda)^2}P_0 + \left(\dfrac{1}{\mu}\right) \quad = \quad \frac{10\left(\dfrac{7.5}{10}\right)^2}{(20-7.5)^2}0.4545 + 0.10$$

$$= \quad \left(\frac{5.625}{156.25}\right)0.4545 + 0.10 \quad = \quad 0.12 \text{ hours, or about 7 minutes}$$

Finally, we can calculate the average time a car spends waiting:

$$T_w \quad = \quad T_S - \frac{1}{\mu} \quad = \quad 0.12 - 0.10 = 0.02 \text{ hours, or roughly 1 minute.}$$

Clearly, adding a second crew would dramatically improve customer service. Luc will need to consider the additional cost of providing this extra capacity, and what impact, if any, it will have on overall demand.

****

B.2 SIMULATION MODELING

APICS defines simulation as "the technique of using representative or artificial data to reproduce in a model various conditions that are likely to occur in the actual performance of a system."[1] Although simulations can include physical recreations of an actual system, most business simulations are computer-based and use mathematical formulas to represent actual systems or policies. Simulation models have a number of advantages:

1. **Off-line evaluation of new processes or process changes.** Simulation models allows the user to experiment with processes or operating procedures without endangering the performance of real-world systems. For example, the user can test new systems or evaluate the impact of changes to processes or procedures prior to implementing them.

---

[1] Cox, J. F., and J. H. Blackstone (eds.). *APICS Dictionary*, 10th ed. Falls Church, VA: APICS (2002).

2. **Time compression.** Simulation models allow the user to compress time. Many days, months, or even years of activity can be simulated in a short period of time.

3. **"What if" analsyses.** This can be particularly valuable in understanding how processes or procedures would perform under extreme conditions. What if the demand rate was to double? What if one of our key support centers was down? With simulation models, managers can get an idea of the impact prior to an actual occurence.

Of course, simulations have their disadvantages:

1. **It is still a simulation.** Most simulation models – like the waiting line formulas we reviewed in the first half of the supplement – make simplifying assumptions about how the real-world works. While these assumptions make the model easier to develop and understand, they also make it less realistic.

2. **The more realistic a simulation model is, the more costly it will be to develop and the more difficult it will be to interpret.** This is the converse of the first point. Model developers must strike a balance between cost, ease of use, and realism.

3. **Simulation models do not provide an"optimal" solution.** Simulation models only reflect the conditions and rules of the environments they are set up to model.

Monte Carlo Simulation

By far the most common form of simulation modeling is mathematical simulation, where mathematical formulas and statistical processes are used to simulate activities, decisions, and the like. One particularly well-known approach is **Monte Carlo simulation**, a technique in which statistical sampling is used to generate outcomes for a large number of trials. The results of these trials are then used evaluated to gain insight into the system of interest.

Monte Carlo simulation is used to simulate all types of systems and many types of statistical distributions. To illustrate the basic principles of the technique, we will take a very simple system everyone is familiar with: Flipping a coin. You probably understand that for a fair coin, each outcome – heads or tails – has a 50% chance of occurring. And you probably also understand that the outcome for any particular flip is **memoryless**; that is, the probability of coming up heads or tails is unaffected by what happened previously. Still, you may wonder how the pattern of outcomes might play out over, say, fifty flips.

Figure B.4 shows an Excel-based Monte Carlo simulation model for 50 coin flips, or trials. The random numbers for the 50 trials were generated using the following Excel formula:

=RAND()*100

This formula generates a random number between 0 and 100, with all numbers having an equal probability of being generated. The adjacent column in the spreadsheet then translates these results into heads or tails. For example:

Formula for Cell C6: =IF(B6<50,"Tails", "Heads")

Translated, if the random number in Cell B6 is less than 50, write "Tails" in the cell; otherwise, write "Heads." Looking at the results, we can see that "Tails" came up 27 times and "Heads" came up 23 times – not exactly a 50/50 balance, but close. In addition, we can see that the simulated results do not alternate back and forth between heads and tails. In fact, there are several runs of four or more heads or tails.

Figure B.4: Excel-based Monte Carlo simulation of 50 coin tosses

	A	B	C	D	E	F	G
1	Monte Carlo simulation of 50 coin tosses						
2	Excel-generated random numbers generated between 0 and 100						
3	"Tails" if random number < 50, "Heads" otherwise						
4							
5	Trial	Random Number	Simulated Outcome		Trial	Random Number	Simulated Outcome
6	1	75.79	Heads		26	41.23	Tails
7	2	54.88	Heads		27	28.41	Tails
8	3	3.20	Tails		28	80.16	Heads
9	4	89.32	Heads		29	79.27	Heads
10	5	64.62	Heads		30	6.34	Tails
11	6	25.56	Tails		31	89.72	Heads
12	7	60.99	Heads		32	14.85	Tails
13	8	77.68	Heads		33	15.76	Tails
14	9	77.14	Heads		34	99.29	Heads
15	10	51.42	Heads		35	40.66	Tails
16	11	14.43	Tails		36	19.91	Tails
17	12	27.02	Tails		37	55.73	Heads
18	13	25.73	Tails		38	83.07	Heads
19	14	43.28	Tails		39	69.75	Heads
20	15	36.91	Tails		40	14.89	Tails
21	16	49.08	Tails		41	45.60	Tails
22	17	88.84	Heads		42	0.40	Tails
23	18	45.94	Tails		43	80.11	Heads
24	19	97.69	Heads		44	16.58	Tails
25	20	27.94	Tails		45	19.35	Tails
26	21	78.90	Heads		46	15.19	Tails
27	22	90.03	Heads		47	32.78	Tails
28	23	64.11	Heads		48	25.08	Tails
29	24	60.71	Heads		49	95.15	Heads
30	25	2.02	Tails		50	45.36	Tails

Monte Carlo simulation can be used to simulate other statistical distributions as well. Figure B.5 shows another Excel-based Monte Carlo simulation model. In this case, we are trying to simulate arrivals, based on a Poisson distribution and an average arrival rate per time period of 3.

First, the spreadsheet calculates the probability of 0 through 8 arrivals per time period using Equation [B-1]. Notice that the total of these probabilities is essentially 100%. Next, we assigned random numbers between 0 and 100 to each possible arrival quantity. For example, there is a 5% chance of 0 arrivals. Therefore, we assigned all numbers (r) which meet the condition ($0 \leq r < 5$) to represent 0 arrivals. Since the probability of drawing such a number using the "=RAND()*100" equation is also 5%, we can use this method to accurately simulate Poisson-distributed arrivals. Arrivals of 1 through 8 units per time period were simulated in a similar fashion.

The bottom half of Figure B.5 presents results for 20 simulated time periods. Notice how the simulated arrivals range anywhere from 0 to 8. For this particular simulation, the average arrival rate is 3.1, close to the expected arrival rate of 3 per time period. $T = 1$ in this example.

Figure B.5: Excel-based Monte Carlo simulation of Poisson-distributed arrivals

Monte Carlo simulation of Poisson-distributed arrivals				
Arrival rate (λ) =	3			
Arrivals	Probability of n arrivals	Cumulative probability	Assigned random numbers (r) (0 to 100)	
0	5%	5%	$0 \le r < 5$	
1	15%	20%	$5 \le r < 20$	
2	22%	42%	$20 \le r < 42$	
3	22%	65%	$42 \le r < 65$	
4	17%	82%	$65 \le r < 82$	
5	10%	92%	$82 \le r < 92$	
6	5%	97%	$92 \le r < 9$	
7	2%	99%	$97 \le r < 99$	
8	1%	100%	99 or greater	
Time Period	Random no.	Simulated Arrivals		
1	75.60	4		
2	74.03	4		
3	80.70	4		
4	22.18	2		
5	88.12	5		
6	75.95	4		
7	47.38	3		
8	10.63	1		
9	34.96	2		
10	42.99	3		
11	83.14	5		
12	2.68	0		
13	8.21	1		
14	73.41	4		
15	39.71	2		
16	73.79	4		
17	99.70	8		
18	22.89	2		
19	19.32	1		
20	64.51	3		
	Average:	3.1		

Building and Evaluating Simulation Models with SimQuick

Developing a useful simulation model can require a great deal of creativity and practice, but the basic process can be divided into four steps:

1. Develop a picture of the system to be modeled. The process mapping material in Chapter 3 of the book can be particularly helpful in this regard.

2. Identify the objects, elements, and probability distributions that define the system. **Objects** are the people or products that move through the system, while **elements** are pieces of the system itself, such as lines, work stations, and entrance and exit points.

3. Determine the experimental conditions and required outputs. Many simulation packages provide the user with options regarding the output reports that are generated.

4. Build and test the simulation model for your system, and capture and evaluate the relevant data.

When the process to be modeled is fairly complex, it usually makes sense to use a specialized simulation software package. These packages can range from very sophisticated applications that provide graphics and sophisticated "what if" analyses and make use of existing company databases, to simple stand-alone package. In the following example, we build and test a simulation model of Luc's Deluxe Car Wash using SimQuick[2], a highly-intuitive, easy-to-learn simulation package that runs under Microsoft Excel.

****

Boxed Example B.4: Simulating operations at Luc's Deluxe Car Wash

While Luc is generally happy with the statistics he was able to generate using the waiting line formulas (Examples B.1 – B.3), one thing troubles him: All of these statistics describe *averages* – average wait time, average number of cars in the system, and so on. They don't tell Luc how long the lines can actually get, or what the maximum time might look like.

Luc's car wash is pictured in Figure B.6. For simulation modeling purposes, there are four elements that make up Luc's car wash: The entrance, driveway (which serves as a buffer point), the crew, and washed cars. Two of these elements – cars arriving and the crews washingn cars – are controlled by probability distributions.

---

[2] Hartvigsen, D., <u>SimQuick: Process Simulation in Excel. Prentice-Hall</u>. 1st Edition, 2001.

Figure B.6: Luc's Car Wash

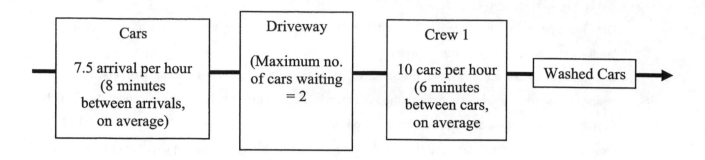

Figure B.7 shows how the same system is defined in SimQuick. The first box is labeled "simulation controls." Luc has set the simulation to cover five iterations of 3600 minutes each. In effect, *each* iteration represents a work-week consisting of five 12-hour days. The fact that Luc can run our simulation in a matter of seconds illustrates the time compression advantages of simulation.

The simulation model has one entrance point, "Cars." Cars arrive following an exponential distribution, with an average of 8 minutes between arrivals. Note that this is the *same* as saying that the arrivals are Poisson-distributed with an average of $\dfrac{60 \text{ minutes}}{8 \text{ minutes}} = 7.5$ arrivals per hour.

Once a car "arrives", it then goes to the driveway, which is the first buffer point in the model. For now, Luc assumes that there is unlimited room for cars to wait here ("Capacity ➜ 10000"). If the washing crew is not busy, the car will immediately proceed to the workstation "Crew 1." Otherwise it will wait in the driveway.

The earlier examples stated that a crew can wash, on average, 10 cars per hour. This is the same as saying that the time between successive washed cars is 6 minutes, on average ("Exp(6)"). Once a car is finished, it proceeds to the "Washed Cars" buffer. By modeling the system this way, Luc can track how many cars are completed by the end of each iteration.

Figure B.7: SimQuick Model Specification for Single-Channel, Single-Phase System, Luc's Deluxe Car Wash

	A	B	C	D	E	F
1	**Model View**					
2	(Note: Cannot edit model here)					
3						
4		Simulation controls:				
5						
6		Time units per simulation →	3600			
7		Number of simulations →	5			
8						
9						
10		Entrances:				
11						
12		1				
13		Name →	Cars			
14		Time between arrivals →	Exp(8)			
15		Num. objects per arrival →	1			
16		Output				
17		destination(s) ↓				
18		Driveway				
19						
20						
21						
22		Work Stations:				
23						
24			1			
25			Name →	Crew 1		
26			Working time →	Exp(6)		
27		Output	# of output	Resource	Resource	
28		destination(s) ↓	objects ↓	name(s) ↓	# units needed ↓	
29		Washed Cars	1			
30						
31						
32						
33		Buffers:				
34						
35		1			2	
36		Name →	Driveway		Name →	Washed Cars
37		Capacity →	10000		Capacity →	10000
38		Initial # objects →	0		Initial # objects →	0
39		Output	Output		Output	Output
40		destination(s) ↓	group size ↓		destination(s) ↓	group size ↓
41		Crew 1	1			
42						

Figure B.8 shows the overall simulation results for five simulations of 3600 minutes each (five workweeks, each consisting of five 12-hour days).

Figure B.8: Simulation results for Single-Channel, Single-Phase System

Results							
Element names	**Statistics**	**Overall means**	**Simulation Numbers**				
			1	**2**	**3**	**4**	**5**
Cars	Objects entering process	447.40	460	471	460	424	422
	Objects unable to enter	0.00	0	0	0	0	0
	Service level	1.00	1.00	1.00	1.00	1.00	1.00
Crew 1	Final status	NA	Working	Working	Working	Working	Working
	Final inventory (int. buff.)	0.00	0	0	0	0	0
	Mean inventory (int. buff.)	0.00	0.00	0.00	0.00	0.00	0.00
	Mean cycle time (int. buff.)	0.00	0.00	0.00	0.00	0.00	0.00
	Work cycles started	444.20	459	466	453	421	422
	Fraction time working	0.77	0.77	0.81	0.79	0.75	0.73
	Fraction time blocked	0.00	0.00	0.00	0.00	0.00	0.00
Driveway	Objects leaving	444.20	459	466	453	421	422
	Final inventory	3.20	1	5	7	3	0
	Minimum inventory	0.00	0	0	0	0	0
	Maximum inventory	15.80	13	21	22	13	10
	Mean inventory	2.58	2.07	3.74	3.84	1.75	1.47
	Mean cycle time	20.64	16.22	28.89	30.55	15.01	12.54
Washed Cars	Objects leaving	0.00	0	0	0	0	0
	Final inventory	443.20	458	465	452	420	421
	Minimum inventory	0.00	0	0	0	0	0
	Maximum inventory	443.20	458	465	452	420	421
	Mean inventory	219.71	233.76	228.58	223.11	196.72	216.40
	Mean cycle time	Infinite	Infinite	Infinite	Infinite	Infinite	Infinite

Statistics regarding wait times and waiting line lengths can be found by looking at the "Driveway." Results. In this case, "inventory" represents cars waiting to be washed. The average inventory is 2.58 cars and the mean cycle (ie, waiting) time is 20.64 minutes. It's interesting to comparing the simulation results to the formula-derived results in Example B.1:

Formula-derived estimate of average

number of cars waiting (C_w)   =   *2.25 cars*

Simulation estimate of average number of cars waiting   =   *2.58 cars*

Formula-derived estimate of average waiting time (T_w) = 0.3 hours, or about *18 minutes*

Simulation estimate of average number of cars waiting   =   *20.64 minutes*

Figure B.8 also shows the average maximum number of cars in line across all five simulations was 15.8, and the fraction of time the washing crew was busy was 0.77, or 77%.
****

****

Boxed Example B.5: Simulating the impact of limited waiting space at Luc's Deluxe Car Wash

Satisfied that the simulation model adequately reflects his business, Luc decides to modify the model to capture one key characteristic that has not yet been considered. Specifically, *there is only enough room in the driveway for two cars to be waiting*. This means that if the crew is busy washing a car and two cars are already waiting, any other car that drives up will have to go elsewhere. Luc wonders how this would affect the results.

The modified simulation model is identical to the one shown in Figure B.7, except now the capacity for the driveway buffer is set at 2. Simulation results for this new model are shown in Figure B.9.

Figure B.9: Simulation results for Single-Channel, Single-Phase System – Driveway capacity is limited to 2 cars

Results							
Element names	**Statistics**	**Overall means**	**Simulation Numbers**				
			1	**2**	**3**	**4**	**5**
Cars	Objects entering process	378.20	386	376	373	396	360
	Objects unable to enter	61.40	65	49	62	68	63
	Service level	0.86	0.86	0.88	0.86	0.85	0.85
Crew 1	Final status	NA	Working	Working	Not Working	Working	Not Working
	Final inventory (int. buff.)	0.00	0	0	0	0	0
	Mean inventory (int. buff.)	0.00	0.00	0.00	0.00	0.00	0.00
	Mean cycle time (int. buff.)	0.00	0.00	0.00	0.00	0.00	0.00
	Work cycles started	377.60	384	376	373	395	360
	Fraction time working	0.64	0.65	0.60	0.61	0.69	0.63
	Fraction time blocked	0.00	0.00	0.00	0.00	0.00	0.00
Driveway	Objects leaving	377.60	384	376	373	395	360
	Final inventory	0.60	2	0	0	1	0
	Minimum inventory	0.00	0	0	0	0	0
	Maximum inventory	2.00	2	2	2	2	2
	Mean inventory	0.49	0.53	0.40	0.43	0.59	0.51
	Mean cycle time	4.68	4.93	3.85	4.12	5.41	5.10
Washed Cars	Objects leaving	0.00	0	0	0	0	0
	Final inventory	377.00	383	375	373	394	360
	Minimum inventory	0.00	0	0	0	0	0
	Maximum inventory	377.00	383	375	373	394	360
	Mean inventory	187.57	194.89	188.37	188.99	195.84	169.77
	Mean cycle time	Infinite	Infinite	Infinite	Infinite	Infinite	Infinite

Looking at the results, Luc can clearly see the impact the small driveway is having on his business. According to the simulation results, on average, 61.4 cars per day are unable to enter the process. Because fewer cars enter the system, the fraction of time the washing crew is busy also suffers. In fact, it drops down to 64%. Finally, the mean time and mean number of cars in the driveway decrease dramatically, but this is only because a large number of cars are *turned away*. In Theory of Constraints terms (Chapter 8), the driveway is clearly a constraint that limits throughput for the entire system. If Luc can somehow find more space to queue up the cars, he could expect to achieve results closer to those in Figure B.8.

****

SUPPLEMENT SUMMARY

In this supplement, we described different types of waiting line systems. We also provided formulas for evaluating the steady-state performance of three different systems. The second half of the supplement introduced simulation modeling, including a discussion and examples of Monte Carlo simulation, as well as the development and analysis of a simulation model using SimQuick.

Simulation modeling is a particularly important tool that managers can use to model and gain insight into complex business processes. Simulation is often the only way managers can understand what impact changes in capacity, process flows, or other elements of the business will have on customer performance.

We encourage you not to let your education end here, however. There is much more to both of these topics, and especially simulation modeling, than can be covered in this supplement. In fact, there are books devoted to simulation modeling[3], and many colleges offer courses or even series of courses on the topic.

DISCUSSION QUESTIONS

1. All things being equal, why do you think waiting line environments with constant service times have shorter waiting times and lines? Can you think of an example to illustrate your intuition?

2. Consider a supply chain where multiple manufacturers take turns processing a particular product. Which of the waiting line systems shown in Figures B.1 – B.3 best represent this environment? Explain.

3. We stated earlier that simulation modeling does not provide the user with an optimal solution. What did we mean by this? Explain, using one or more of the simulation examples given in the supplement.

---

[3] See for example, Banks, J., Carson, J., Nelson, B. and Nicol, D. Discrete-Event System Simulation, Prentice-Hall, 3rd Edition, 2004.

PROBLEMS

Additional homework problems are available at http://www.prenhall.com/bozarth. These problems use Excel to generate customized problems for different class sections or even different students.

(* = easy; ** = moderate; *** = advanced)

1. Horton Williams Airport is a small municipal airport with two runways. One of these runways is devoted just to planes taking off. During peak time periods, about 8.5 planes per hour radio to the tower that they want to take off. The tower handles these requests in the order they arrive. Once the tower has given the go-ahead, it take the plane, on average, 5 minutes to position itself on the runway and take-off.

   a. (*) On average, how many planes will be waiting during peak time periods? How many will be in the system (waiting and on the runway)?

   b. (*) How long, on average, will a plane have to wait before it is allowed to take off?

2. The Women's department at Hector's Department Store has a single checkout register. Customers arrive at the register at the rate of 11 per hour. It takes the clerk, on average, 4 minutes to check out a customer.

   a. (**) On average, how many customers will be waiting to be check out? In your mind, is this number reasonable? Why or why not?

   b. (**) How long, on average, will a customer have to wait before the clerk starts serving them? Again, is this a reasonable time? If Hector's decides to open another register, what are the trade-offs to consider?

3. Parts arrive at an automated machining center at the rate of 100 per hour, based on a Poisson distribution. The machining center is able to process these parts at a fixed rate of 150 per hour. That is, each part will take exactly 150/6 = 0.4 minutes to process.

   a. (*) How many parts, on average, will be waiting to be processed? How many will be in the system (waiting and being processed)?

   b. (*) How long, on average, will a part have to wait before it is processed?

4. To deal with greater demand, Horton Williams Airport (Problem 1) has opened up a second runway devoted just to planes taking off. Peak demand has now been bumped up to 15 planes per hour. Furthermore, each plane still takes about 5 minutes to position itself and take off, once it has been given the go-ahead.

    a. (***) On average, how many planes will be waiting during peak time periods? How many will be in the system (waiting and on the runway)?

    b. (***) How long, on average, will a plane have to wait before it is allowed to take off?

5. Hector's Department store (Problem 2) has decided to add a second checkout register. This second register works at the same average speed as the first. Customer arrivals are the same as before.

    a. (***) On average, how many customers will be waiting to be check out? From a business perspective, is this reasonable?

    b. (***) How long, on average, will a customer have to wait before the clerk starts serving them? Again, is this a reasonable time?

6. Consider the Monte Carlo simulation shown in Figure B.5.

    a. (**) Recalculate the values in the "Probability of n arrivals" and "Cumulative probability" columns for an arrival rate of 4. You may need to add some additional rows beyond just 8 arrivals.

    b. (**) Based on the results to Part a., redo the assigned random numbers column.

    c. (**) Using the same random numbers shown in Figure B.5, take the results from Parts a and b, and redo the column labeled "Simulated arrivals." What is the new average number of arrivals per time period?

7. Consider the SimQuick simulation model for Luc's Car Wash, shown in Figure B.6. Suppose Luc decides to put in place a second crew. Redraw Figure B.6 to reflect this change. What changes to the model specification (Figure B.7) would you need to make? (Hint: You will not only need to make changes to the work stations, but to the "Driveway" buffer as well).

REFERENCES

Banks, J., Carson, J., Nelson, B. and Nicol, D. <u>Discrete-Event System Simulation,</u> Prentice-Hall, 3rd Edition. 2004.

Hartvigsen, D., <u>SimQuick: Process Simulation in Excel. Prentice-Hall</u>. 1st Edition, 2001.